Restoring your inner child: A simple guide on how to restore your wholeness

Nicole M. Phillips

Table of content

Chapter 1

Locating and reestablishing a connection with your inner child

Our inner child is a part of us that has existed since conception, throughout infancy, and all the years that followed when we were growing up and becoming our most vulnerable selves: baby, infant, toddler, young child, and middle school.

The inner child frequently remembers both positive and negative events from their childhood, including neglect, trauma, and significant loss. When we begin to explore our inner world, it can be challenging to identify the precise event that is pulling at us. However, we can begin to notice our internal patterns that have subconsciously left us with "bread crumb trails."

We all have a "inner child" that lives inside of us.
You possess a child inside. I have a child inside me. All of us do. Your subconscious has been receiving messages from your "inner child" long before it was able to fully comprehend what was happening (mentally and emotionally). It contains hopes and dreams for the future as well as feelings, memories, and beliefs from the past.

When you explain inner child work and how we all have a little one (or little ones) inside of us, people are always fascinated and excited. We frequently observe a shift in our clients' healing and general improvement toward clarity of the self and greater treatment progress when we create space for inner child healing.

Our inner child's needs, pains, hopes, and dreams are often neglected as we get older in order to conform to society's expectations of who we should be. When we are young, reality and fantasy collide like carefree watercolors because we are not concerned with what is real and what is not. The last time we play is one day. In order to make room for our adult lives and the various expectations we must fulfill in order to be accepted, we neglect our inner child.

According to Dr. Venetia Leonidaki, "We need to strike a balance between the emotional needs we feel internally and the demands made or restrictions imposed by other people around us from an early age. We are expected to act responsibly, restrain our emotions, be logical, and adhere to societal norms by our parents, teachers, and later, our partners, employers, and children. We frequently end up stifling and cutting off from our inner child because we have to constantly balance our needs internally with pressures from the outside world.

"We often ignore our inner child out of a desire to please others and a concern that we will lose their affection if we don't. A part is also played by neurobiology. New degrees of complexity in our thinking are brought about by changes in specific brain regions, such as the prefrontal cortex, which better equips us to control our emotions and impulses. Our most developed, adult reasoning abilities may cause us to depend less on the raw emotions that our inner child is most in touch with, alienating us from the infantile side of ourselves.

What aspects of our inner child can we recognize?
The part of us that still feels like a kid recalls how grandmother smelled when she knelt down to give us a hug and how proud she looked at us when we showed her how we could ride a bike.

When we shared our favorite toy with the neighbor, our inner child recalls how our hearts were filled with happiness and love and our father's eyes glistened as he gazed at us.

Our inner kid recalls being delighted and self-assured when they received an invitation to a friend's birthday celebration.

Our inner kid is also the one who experienced the salty tears streaming down our cheeks as our mother hurriedly left the home to go say goodbye to her father while he was dying.

On the bus on the first day of school, our inner child recalls being shunned and harassed.

When the instructor mocked at us or when we didn't have the solution to a "apparently simple" question, our inner child likely recalls feeling stupid.

When we start our first work, our inner kid is there to show your manager that you're competent and responsible while also making them feel proud.

When we are teens, we have an inner kid that yearns to fit in.
When we search for love or want to join certain social circles, we are searching for our inner child.

When we enjoy ourselves with others, it's the part of us that feels peaceful, understood, and cozy.

It is also the area that is crushed and feels betrayed when we are lied to, disregarded, or mistreated in any other way.

We only need to learn to listen to our inner kid, who is always speaking to us.
Now, our inner kid may either be peaceful and satisfied (for the most part) or it can misbehave and make things a little tense within, getting in the way of good relationships, organizational abilities, and self control.

When it comes to becoming a contributing member of society or taking the necessary efforts to achieve happiness, our inner child may make or break it.

Your inner kid probably needs some care if you're feeling trapped or irritated in any area of your life. Stuck spots might manifest as challenges in the workplace, with parenting, falling in love or staying in love, building stronger connections, or establishing boundaries.

When the inner child takes over

Your fear, perfectionism, anxiety, or avoidance of certain people, places, or events may become apparent. All of these are attempts by your inner kid to feel secure. When the inner child is in charge, it will make decisions based on unconscious assumptions or old experiences as well as on what it feels it needs to feel secure.

The inner child often lacks access to the reality of the adult "self" and may not be aware of how life is different today or how things have changed.

Childhood emotional scars might make you feel like you're carrying around a heavy load.

You can feel as if you are carrying the weight of the whole world on your shoulders if your inner kid is dragging 50 pounds of misery around with them. It could prevent you from making changes if your inner child experienced instability, unpredictability, or danger. You could notice a scared aspect of yourself that prevents you from attempting new things, but if you want to go on with your life, you'll probably feel conflicted.

We get trapped when we have conflicting needs for potential, connection, and adventure. One side wants safety and predictability.

You can "unstuck" so that you can go over obstacles and reach a middle ground. It will be crucial for your adult self and kid self to get to

It will be crucial for your adult self and kid self to get to know one another in order to build the balance of creativity, flexibility, responsibility, connectedness, and consistency. This is the first stage in building a cohesive team where both your adult demands and inner child needs are satisfied.

How to Devclop a Relationship with Your Inner Child in Two Easy Steps

Here, two stages are crucial:

One: Connecting with your inner child, having a conversation with it, and becoming close to it.

TWO: Taking measures to realize your inner child's needs, sorrows, desires, and goals by starting to actually listen to them.

Get in touch with your inner child with the help of our meditation on connecting with your inner child. Our goal is for you to become aware of how your inner child is doing, to provide it some compassionate care, and to discover a means to accommodate its requirements. When you do this, it often becomes clearer what needs to change so that you may advance. Additionally, the resistance and "stuckness" you experience throughout your adult life are often softened by this internal process.

Some people find that "reparenting" their inner child is also beneficial in this process.)

gaining access to one's inner child to lift burdens and to inspire hope and pleasure.
Start here.
We start by asking your adult self to be a bit vulnerable and transparent in order to do this. We need to be receptive to hearing and witnessing the tale of our inner child; inquiring about its existence, its goals, aspirations, concerns, and anxieties in order for it to come out of hiding and speak about what is happening or what it needs.

In order for your inner child to be able to freely communicate, we want it to start building a trustworthy connection with your adult self. As well as its suffering, misery, anxieties, and concerns, we want to know about its hopes, dreams, desires, and words.

We often see that the inner child may settle down and experience the emotions that it had to suppress for years when it has someone (the adult you) who really cares, slows down, and is there with it. As this work may be delicate, it is often advised to work with a qualified therapist who specializes in inner child work, childhood emotional maltreatment, or emotional difficulties. A good clinician can assist you through the work and support your recovery.

It is unexpected to learn how much our current level of pleasure depends on events from our past, namely from our childhood. You will be one step closer to living a happy life if you use your early experiences as a road map for the future and acknowledge the influence the past has on your present. How well-adjusted you are and how you make decisions depend on how you were raised and the relationships you had during those crucial early years.

Your cheerful, joyous, emotional, free, playful inner child is a strong aspect of your psyche. It mixes your most primal emotions, your sensitivity and creativity that you were born with but may have repressed as you grew older, and it symbolizes the little kid you once were that needed love and care.

The inner child, or childlike side of humanity, is influenced by all you learnt and experienced as a child before puberty. Being aware of your inner kid, which is a semi-independent being subservient to your conscious mind, may help you live a better life. Your true self is the innocent, carefree, and fun part of your awareness—your inner child.

Learn how to access your inner child

You may have a happy and healthy life by learning how to tap into your inner child. You have the ability to increase your emotional freedom and find greater inner peace when you look for your inner child. Discovering your inner child will make you feel happier, more energetic, and even transform the way you see certain unquestionable things. This sort of profound spiritual connection influences all aspect of your life. Here are few easy steps:

1. Stop limiting your activities - Always think about how impulsive you were as a

youngster vs today. Try to pay attention to the voice inside of you telling you to try something new rather than dismissing it. Allowing novelty into your life and letting go of daily restrictions can allow you to freely explore new hobbies and sensations.

2. Explore your imagination - Permit yourself to be creative on a regular basis, in both your actions and thoughts. Instead of obsessing about what other people think, wish, or expect of you, utilize your inspiration to uncover fresh opportunities for pleasure.

3. Improve your listening abilities - When trying to become better at listening, remember to start with the tiniest of things, such as the sound of your own heartbeat. Next, begin to listen to the noises in your immediate

environment and determine their significance for you. Your world is sending you crucial signals, so focus your heart and intellect on them.

4. Embrace the spirit energy - By doing this, you will be allowing the energy to flow and improving your awareness of your inner voice. Making judgments at the appropriate time and place may be aided by this. Additionally, it might help you attract the right individuals and foster synchronicity in your life.

5. Take a moment to grin and laugh - Everyone has difficulties in life, but that doesn't mean you shouldn't look for reasons to laugh. Be thankful for your experiences each day and keep an eye out for new things to do to spice up your life.

6. Engage your senses in the world - Just go back to when you were younger and the world appeared more colorful. Those pictures ought to make you remember how happy you were when you had a more positive outlook on life. You should take some time to savor the details, like the hues of the street you walk on every day, the aroma of the newly-baked pie, or the texture of the new outfit you just purchased.

Five ways to embrace your inner kid

Here are five methods to open your heart with love and compassion to your inner child if you're prepared to do so.

1. Be imaginative. Any creative endeavor or game asks us to use our imagination, let down our guard, and engage our emotions. You might experiment with

anything, such as painting, pantomime, or karaoke singing. Our childish traits, such as spontaneity, playfulness, inventiveness, and having fun, are unlocked by creative activities.

2. Interaction with kids. You may experience firsthand a carefree but yet intensely emotional state of being by spending meaningful time with youngsters, particularly your own children. Additionally, it could make it simpler for you to recall emotions and experiences from your own childhood.

3. Discovering love. Of course, we can't prepare for this, but when we fall in love, we will undoubtedly feel a variety of feelings, some of which may be comparable to those we had as kids. When we fall in love, we experience a variety of powerful emotional states that

are closely related to those we experienced as children, including an increased desire for affection and intimacy, feelings of jealously, and separation anxiety.

4. Draw on your early recollections. Close your eyes and let your thoughts wander to childhood recollections. These memories may be recalled more vividly when you pay attention to sensory aspects. How did we appear? Any scents that come to mind? This work may also be aided by looking back at old pictures, finding old toys, or visiting areas we used to frequent as kids.

5. Consult a counselor. Having a therapist to lead us through this process may be quite useful. A therapist may be helpful by bringing to light any subdued or hidden feelings that may be associated

with this aspect of yourself. Some therapists may use experiential methods to release your inner child. One such method is called "chairwork," when you are urged to sit on a chair and speak as your younger self while doing so.

It is a powerful experience that reveals a lot about ourselves, our emotions, and our quest for happiness to bring out our inner child, nurture it, and make an effort to connect with it.

Even though you may not give them much thought right now, when you go through this process of discovery, you could learn that there are still old scars from the past that have not fully healed. It's crucial to have your mental wounds healed so that you can guide your inner child and yourself along a healthier path.

The emotional scars you experienced as a youngster might deepen with time. As you age, you could develop emotional sensitivity and problematic behavior. Low self-esteem, emotional imbalances, eating disorders, identity challenges, problems with relationships, and even drug and alcohol addictions and criminal behavior are examples of symptoms.

The inner kid exists in everyone, but not everyone understands how to interact with them. Recognizing them, accepting their presence with self-compassion, and allowing them to occupy space in your adult life is the first step in the journey of self-discovery. Healing your inner child will enable you to find the root of many worries, insecurities, and destructive life patterns, and will be the only path to true pleasure. Here are a few actions that may assist you in that endeavor. You can only empower yourself to live a better life by connecting with your inner child and expressing love.

By consciously acknowledging this aspect of ourselves, we may start to identify the limiting beliefs that date back to our early years and are responsible for how we respond to certain individuals or circumstances. Everyone has an inner kid, but as we grow up, many of us unconsciously cut those ties.

When our needs as children aren't satisfied, our inner child feels hurt, and the ensuing behavioral patterns may have an influence on our self-esteem in adulthood, resulting in unsatisfying romantic relationships or the emergence of self-destructive life habits.

Chapter 2

Reparenting yourself and escaping the toxic parenting of your youth

Although we don't discuss physical punishment much anymore, it used to be a common practice in parenting. Physical punishment is not prevalent in practice, even though public opinion may have silenced the discussion. According to a 2013 Harris Poll, two-thirds of parents admitted to using physical punishment on their kids and 81 percent of parents think that beating is sometimes appropriate.

The threat of spanking was a common refrain in American families until the 1980s as a means of controlling children. And what about the verbal beating that came after a task that was done carelessly? Yes, that was an improvement over the belt. Although these parenting techniques weren't classified as abuse, scientific data suggests otherwise.

Hard physical and verbal punishments have often been demonstrated in studies to be ineffective, dangerous, and capable of causing behavioral and physical issues that last into adulthood. Why, in light of all the facts, do individuals continue to engage in it?

Research by the Social Development Research Group at the University of Washington found that individuals who experienced physical and mental abuse as children are more likely to replicate such behaviors with their kids. The scientists identified regular instances of bad parenting spanning three generations, including physical and mental abuse, which suggests that such decisions might have a long-lasting impact on families.

According to Susan Newman, a social psychologist and the author of "Nobody's Baby Now: Reinventing Your Relationship with Your Mother and Father," parents who are willing to break the pattern with their children confront a challenging route.

If you've experienced abuse, you could start abusing others, warns Newman. It's similar to alcoholism in that youngsters are more prone to start drinking if there is a lot of drinking in the home.

Change is possible, however challenging it may be. Here are some ideas on how parents may stop abusive behaviors and communicate differently with their children.

Recognize your mistreatment. Recognizing the abuse is the first, and maybe most challenging, step in ending the cycle of abuse in families. The issue of discipline is one of culture: The approaches that are deemed appropriate change depending on when and where you were raised. It's important, according to Newman, to reflect on the past with objectivity. The ability to separate apart what you see as detrimental or destructive habits so you don't pass them on to your children comes with becoming an adult, according to the author. She also advises against burying unpleasant feelings by adopting the attitude that "it doesn't matter; I came out OK." The agony they are experiencing won't go away, according to Newman, and it will show out in different ways.

Understand the dangers (and ask for help). Trauma often leaves deeper wounds than we are aware of. According to a UCLA study, long-term abuse alters a person's brain's ability to cope with and process stress, as well as the mind and many other bodily systems. The stress that comes with parenting a child with tantrums is well-known. A response to such stress might result in physical abuse of the kid or in what Newman calls "humiliation parenting"—eroding the self-esteem of a child via critical and humiliating speech, often in public.

If you're prone to verbal snarking, Newman advises talking to close friends or your spouse in addition to therapy since it may help you release stress and establish good coping mechanisms.

Set limitations with the elderly. Even with an aggressive parent, cutting off communication may be difficult and uncommon. Even individuals who mentioned emotional abuse, neglect, or traumatic incidents continued to have some kind of contact with their parents, according to a University of Cambridge research on family estrangement. As long as the elder generation respects the limits of their adult offspring, both personally and in terms of their preferred parenting style, having grandparents around may be beneficial for kids. You may cohabit with your parent by telling them, "You had your chance at parenting; this is my turn," or "I know you have the best interests of your grandchild in mind, but we don't agree with that method of doing things," advises Newman. Keep your position strong since you are now your children's parent and their most important role model. What happens if the grandparents don't accept your parental authority? The connection has to be reevaluated, Newman adds.

As success occurs, rejoice. Even in the greatest of circumstances, raising children is difficult, and changing decades of bad parenting practices requires effort and bravery. Celebrating progress, no matter how tiny, can strengthen your relationship with your children and aid in the healing of your terrible past. When you parent well, it gradually helps you regain your self-esteem, according to Newman. It's crucial to tell oneself, "I tried my hardest, I listened to my instincts, and I succeeded. Allow yourself to be proud of choosing a different course.

When you feel exposed, consider your motivations. We all make mistakes as parents, but not all of them have an impact on how our children turn out as adults. But when you're concerned about how your experiences could affect your child's well-being, it can be challenging to make decisions with confidence. Newman advises spending some time to reflect on your motivations if you sense an unmooredness in your words and deeds. Your emotions might become simpler by removing all the annoyance and concentrating on the objective. You won't have an answer if you ask yourself "Why am I hitting my kid?" or "Why am I shouting at my child," according to Newman. "And that's when the transformation starts."

Reparenting Techniques

Social and emotional deficiencies are often carried into adulthood by growing up in an emotionally abusive or dysfunctional environment. Your ability to recover and develop into the emotionally stable adult you want depends on your ability to reparent yourself.

Are you harsh and too critical of yourself?

Or are you being too lax with yourself, failing to establish boundaries, and enabling yourself to engage in risky behavior?

Do you struggle to convey your requirements, control your emotions, or pay little attention to your feelings?

Is it challenging to love and care for yourself?

If so, being self-repairable may be beneficial.

Describe reparenting.
Reparenting is providing your adult self what your parents did not provide for you as a youngster.

More than merely meeting their fundamental requirements, children rely on their parents (food, clothing, and shelter). For instance, we need our parents to help us learn how to create boundaries for ourselves, recognize, express, and control our emotions, as well as how to comfort ourselves, and treat ourselves with kindness.

We're more likely to suffer from these problems as adults if we didn't get age-appropriate punishment, unconditional love, role models for healthy relationships, or the knowledge and abilities to recognize and control our emotions and actions.

Adults often believe that these social and emotional abilities should come naturally to them, yet they have acquired habits. We need loving caregivers, positive role models, and secure chances to practice these life skills (preferably, before we're out in the world on our own) to acquire them.

Sometimes parents arc unable to provide the emotional support we require. They often can't educate us about healthy relationships, respectable boundaries, self-compassion, and respecting our emotions since neither they nor anybody else has ever been taught how. This is often the case in households when there is parental abuse, addiction, or other types of dysfunction, such as Childhood Emotional Neglect (CEN).

Learning these abilities and giving yourself what your parents couldn't is still possible. Between what you need and what your parents can provide, you may make up the difference by providing for yourself.

Develop your repair skills.

By deciding what we need, we can begin reparenting ourselves. What did you not learn as a child? What emotional demands weren't satisfied? We don't always know what we don't know when it comes to these topics; sometimes the answers are evident. Additionally, when you start to rehabilitate yourself and learn more about relationships and emotional wellness, it's natural to find new weaknesses.

The following are some social-emotional abilities and requirements that children often lack:

Communication skills: The capacity for effective and concise expression. the capacity to settle disputes. being forceful as opposed to being aggressive or passive.

Self-care: The capacity to recognize and attend to one's needs. believing that your needs matter and feeling worthy of comfort and attention.

Understanding and accepting your feelings: being able to recognize a variety of emotions and appreciating your emotions.

Resilience: The capacity to bounce back from failures, persevere, and have confidence in oneself.
Being able to manage such situations with maturity and grace; being able to understand that you don't always get what you want and that things don't always go your way (not throwing a tantrum like a toddler).

How exactly do you educate yourself and acquire these skills?

Do as much research as you can on the areas you wish to strengthen. Numerous self-help books are available for purchase or loan from libraries, and there are millions of free self-help articles online.
Look for mentors and instructors. Observing people is another great way to learn. Choose a few individuals in your life who, for instance, have sound

boundaries and control their emotions. Take notes on their actions and words. Ask them for advice on how they establish limits or calm themselves if you're close to them.

Join a 12-step program. Working in a 12-step program like Codependents Anonymous, Alcoholics Anonymous, Adult Children, or Al-Anon may result in significant development and insights into your emotions and decisions.

Visit a counselor. Experts in social and emotional abilities include therapists. They can show you your blind spots and assist you in troubleshooting. They provide a secure setting for learning new skills. Additionally, receiving compassionate, respectful treatment from your therapist who also exhibits acceptance, validation, and emotional control serves as both a corrective experience and a guide for how you should conduct yourself.

Chapter 3

Stages of the recovery process

There are too many situations that your younger self may have absorbed to mention them all. But if you did experience childhood trauma, it's probable that it still affects your life now. These warning indicators point to an inner child that has to be soothed:

Characteristics of a wounded inner child

- Frustration or annoyance
- Strong responses to unfulfilled needs
- Childish outbursts, such as yelling or speaking things out of context
- Expressing frustration at not being understood or feeling heard
- Having trouble expressing yourself or your concerns (alexithymia)
- A low sense of self

The inner child will often be more receptive to you if it knows you are paying attention to it and that you are making every effort to show it love and meet its needs.
It could call for more safety on the physical or emotional levels, greater focus on how you're caring for your mind, body, and soul, the resolution of old wounds, the establishment of personal boundaries, or a change in who you spend time with. Often, this effort will reveal whatever is genuinely significant.

We've seen how many symptoms improve as a result of working with the deeper levels of inner child healing, and clients start moving past and through blocks. We've seen clients start to allow love to actually enter their lives for the first time or to strengthen the love already there. Some people find that by engaging in the deeper work, they are finally able to connect with their children without the irritation they had experienced. Others begin to approach their job and relationships with confidence and become more at ease in their requests for assistance. Others see a significant reduction in the anxiety and terror they were feeling, enabling them to maintain the boundaries they had been attempting to establish for years.

How can you tell whether your inner child is hurting?
feelings of agony, remorse, or humiliation.

persistent overworking and a drive to succeed (to get approval or belonging).
being unable to be in the moment.
regular dread and anxiety

rigid and seeking "perfectness" (cannot handle failure).
having trouble seeing and recognizing "wins" in life (no win will ever be enough).
unhealthy interpersonal behaviors, as well as avoiding love and relationships.
Self-destructive and compulsive behaviour.
Underachieving.
rumination and self-talk that is unpleasant.

Techniques for mending your inner child

To reverse the numbness, use activities to begin feeling (a little bit at a time).
By analyzing traumatic memories or events, work on lowering your anxiety and concerns.

establishing wholesome connections that provide you a sense of security and stability in the world.

establishing a cozy and welcoming atmosphere.

By establishing regular food, sleeping, hygiene, and sexual practices, you may create structure and nutritious self-care.

Establish distinct physical, temporal, emotional, and energy boundaries.

Make hobbies and interests a part of your life by developing them.

Focus should be shifted from performance to doing, being, and celebrating.

Change your internal beliefs (what beliefs you feed yourself, therapy can help with this).

"The inner child represents an emotional state or a way of being, which is a vestige of the kid that we once were," says Dr. Venetia Leonidaki. It is about the part of ourselves that may experience pure delight and be impulsive, playful, and innocent but also feels exposed, is easily wounded or angered, and acts impulsively. We all have a kid portion inside of us since all adults had once been children, but the degree to which each of us experiences this connection varies greatly.

You may explore the aspect of your personality that behaves and feels like a kid by developing a connection with your inner child. Things that occur while you are younger might have an impact on your mental health. Finding and releasing the root reasons of your childhood personality's traits is the main goal of healing your inner child so you may respond to future obstacles in adult life as an adult rather than a wounded kid.

The idea of a "inner child" aids us in better understanding our emotional needs, which are sometimes easily written off as silly and unreasonable. We all have the same fundamental wants as children—for security, affection, approval, independence, spontaneity, and respect for limits.

We still have these requirements as adults, and if they go unfulfilled for a very long period, they may cause a variety of mental health issues. The best opportunity we have to experience a feeling of satisfaction and fulfillment in life is to learn to listen to our inner child, discover methods to nurturc it, and address these essential needs to the greatest extent possible. According to Dr. Venetia Leonidaki, ignoring or being oblivious to our inner child might cause us to feel neglected or disconnected, or it can allow our impulses to take control and result in self-destructive behaviors.

Chapter 4

Releasing the past

How can you let go of past wrongs and move on is a topic that many of us ask ourselves whenever we face heartbreak or emotional distress.

Just as letting go and moving ahead may both be deliberate choices, holding on to the past can also.

Advice on how to let go

Our shared capacity to experience suffering is one characteristic that unites us as humans. We have all experienced suffering, whether it be bodily or mental. How each of us handles that suffering, though, is what makes us unique.

According to experts, it is an indication that we aren't making progress in a growth-oriented method when emotional

suffering hinders us from recovering from a circumstance.
Learning from the experience and focusing on progress and forward motion are two of the finest methods to get beyond hurts. We might get imprisoned in unpleasant sensations and recollections if we become preoccupied with what "could have been."

The following 12 suggestions can assist you in letting go if you're attempting to move on after a traumatic incident but are unsure of where to begin.

1. Develop an uplifting slogan to counter the upsetting ideas
You may either advance or remain stagnant depending on how you speak to yourself. Having a mantra that you repeat to yourself while you're

experiencing emotional distress may often assist you to refocus your thinking. For instance, advises clinical psychologist Carla Manly, Ph.D., try saying, "I can't believe this occurred to me!" rather than becoming caught in it. Try repeating a motivating phrase like "I'm lucky to be able to choose a new route in life that is excellent for me," or anything similar.

2. Establish physical separation

It's typical to hear someone advise that you should keep your distance from the person or circumstance that is upsetting you.

That's not always a terrible notion, says clinical psychologist Ramani Durvasula, Ph.D. For the sheer fact that we are not having to think about it, digest it, or be reminded of it as much, she continues, "creating physical or psychological space between ourselves and the person or circumstance might assist with letting go."

3. Create your art.
It's crucial to put your own needs first. You must decide whether to deal with the pain you've felt. Bring yourself back to the present whenever you consider a person who has hurt you. Then, concentrate on something for which you are thankful.

4. Engage in mindfulness
Marriage and family therapist Lisa Olivera claims that the more present-focused we can be, the less influence our past or future has on us.
Our wounds have less power over us as we begin to practice being present, she continues, and we have more flexibility to decide how we want to react to our life.
5. Treat yourself with kindness.

It's time to be nice and compassionate to yourself if you constantly judge yourself for being unable to let go of a difficult circumstance.

According to Olivera, this entails treating oneself as we would treat a friend, being compassionate toward ourselves, and refraining from making comparisons between our path and that of others.

However, Olivera says, "We may choose to treat ourselves tenderly and compassionately when it arises. Hurt is unavoidable, and we may not be able to escape it.

6. Permit unpleasant feelings to surface.

You're not alone if you avoid experiencing unpleasant feelings out of fear of doing so. In fact, according to Durvasula, individuals often have a fear of emotions like loss, rage, disappointment, or melancholy.

People tend to want to block things out rather than experience them, which might prevent letting go. Durvasula says, "These unpleasant feelings are like riptides. "Allow them to flow from you... Fighting them may leave you stranded, and you could need mental health assistance, the speaker continues.

7. Recognize that the other party may not want to apologize

The healing process will be slowed down if you hold out for the other person to apologize. It's crucial to take care of your recovery if you're in pain or feeling hurt, which can include recognizing that the person who injured you isn't going to apologize.

8. Practice self-care

It often seems like there is nothing but pain when we are injured. According to

Olivera, self-care may take the form of establishing boundaries, saying no, engaging in activities that make us happy and comfortable, and putting our own needs first.

"We become more powerful when we learn to incorporate self-care into our everyday lives. Our hurts don't seem as overpowering when we're at that place, she continues.

9. Surround yourself with positive people.

This simple yet effective advice will help you get through a lot of pain.

Manly says, "We can't do life alone, and we can't even expect ourselves to get over our wounds alone." Allowing ourselves to rely on our loved ones and their support is such a fantastic method to both reduce loneliness and serve as a constant reminder of the positive aspects of our life.

10. Permit yourself to discuss it with others.

It's crucial to permit yourself to speak about difficult emotions or situations that have wounded you.

According to Durvasula, sometimes individuals are unable to move on because they believe they are not permitted to speak about it. She notes that this can be the case if others around them are no longer interested in hearing about it or if the individual concerned is too embarrassed or humiliated to continue talking about it.

But it's crucial to speak things out. Durvasula advises locating a friend or therapist who is kind, patient, and ready to serve as your sounding board in light of this.

11. Permit yourself to be merciful

It may be necessary for you to focus on your forgiveness since waiting for the other person to apologize might prevent you from moving beyond the situation. Because it enables you to let go of any pent-up emotions like resentment, guilt, shame, or grief and move on, forgiveness is essential to the healing process.

12. Look for expert assistance

You may find it helpful to speak with a professional if you're having trouble moving beyond a traumatic event. Sometimes it's difficult to put these suggestions into practice on your own, so you'll need an experienced specialist to assist you.

Advantages to letting go

Make Room for New

When you let go of the past, you start to make room in your life for you to grow and develop into the person you want to be. It will be difficult to forgive yourself if you don't let go of your previous decisions. Make the room you need so that your development may fill it.

Work to Reach Your Goals

Your new objectives can be substantially different from your previous ones. That was anticipated. Focusing on the future will be made easier by letting go of the past. Keep working toward your objectives and keep in mind the course you wish to pursue in life.

Create novel perspectives

You may be more receptive to new lifestyles, viewpoints, and outlooks by letting go of old habits. Your viewpoint will modify along with you. Move through outdated perspectives and toward your objectives.

Accept Better Iterations of Yourself Accept the person you are evolving into. Change takes time and might be unpleasant at times. Consult a mental health expert to help you identify your objectives and the course you wish to pursue in life.

Don't be frightened to develop into your finest self. You have the power to achieve your goals and live the life you've always wanted. You may let go of older versions of yourself by letting go of your history. Growing yourself and embracing a healthier, more productive way of life may feel fantastic.

Chapter 5

Achieving your potential

What exactly does it mean to better oneself? Growth

Some individuals find motivation in the thought of bettering themselves. Others may find it more beneficial to see it as development. Growth is a good thing, but it's not necessarily linear.

The intricacies of improving oneself are unique and might vary from person to person. It demands putting in the time and effort, as well as being prepared to feel uncomfortable.

Everyone aspires to be their best selves, but few succeed in doing so. When it comes to attaining success, pursuing our aspirations, and leading passionate, meaningful lives, we are our own greatest adversaries.

Some of us self-destruct without even recognizing it, while others are aware of it but lack the skills or knowledge to change. However, no matter who you are, 6 fundamental tendencies consistently prevent individuals from succeeding.

20 strategies for improving yourself

1. Make others feel valued
Encouragement and empowerment should always be given.

2. Choose a job you love and dedicate yourself to it.
You won't ever have to work a day in your life if you choose a profession you love.

3. Concentrate on the current task

Make the most of what you have and where you are.

4. Approach each task with the importance
Every task is a reflection of the person who does it.

5. Always act morally, no matter how difficult it may be.
Keep what you can accomplish apart from what you can't.

6. When you can, delegate People perform at their best when you believe in their abilities.

Take the Lead 7.

Do all in your power to push your limitations, even if you're already extremely excellent at your profession.

8. Contribute to the solution
Avoid developing a reputation as a perpetual complainer.

9. Speak Honestly
Let others know that they can rely on you to be sincere, even when doing so presents challenges.

10. Provide as Much Assistance as You Can Along the Way
Become someone who others turn to for help.

11. Never engage in gossip

It should go without saying, but ignore rumors and chitchat.

12. Keep an Upbeat Attitude
Positive thinking spreads quickly.

13. Triple Your Knowledge to Double Your Income
Don't let your abilities and knowledge lapse.

14. Take Emotional Control
Count to 10 when you're enraged, and 100 before you speak.

15. Make Minor Changes Every Day to Achieve Stunning Results

Success often entails several little everyday efforts.

16. Hone Your Talents and Concentrate on Improving Your Skills
Avoid being bored and pick up a new talent to keep yourself competitive.

17. Regardless of the challenges, be an expert at what you do.
Nobody fails who gives it their all.

18. Avoid fostering your fears
Have confidence that you will succeed.

19. Be ready at all times
Success happens when opportunity and readiness collide.

20. Request Assistance When You Need It

There is no such thing as a self-made individual; only with the assistance of others can you succeed in your endeavors.

Chapter 6

Further healing work

A Five-Step Healing Process

First Stage: Grief and Denial

Grief is a strong emotional reaction to the end of a relationship. Desertion and rejection may be the cause. No matter how awful the relationship may have been, there is still a feeling of loss. You will likely deny your loss before learning to accept your pain. "This is not happening to me," you'll think. Denial is a typical human defensive mechanism against difficult-to-accept emotionally upsetting circumstances. It gradually gives way to accepting reality. You'll eventually be able to look at your loss and accept it with strength and increasing hope for the future.

Stage 2: rage

The stage of sorrow and denial is often followed by anger. We question ourselves, "Why me?" at this point. People who have been divorced or separated often shock even themselves with the level of rage they feel at the breakdown of their marriage. Both the spouse and the individual who filed for divorce are experiencing this. Why didn't you listen to me when I informed you we were having trouble is a common thought or emotion. Moving on to the next level is made easier by acknowledging your anger.

Third stage: the negotiating

After managing their anger, a person can believe that if they behave gently, speak politely, or "negotiate," choices might be changed. Sayings like "I promise I won't harm you again if you give me another opportunity" or "I won't go through the divorce if you would just go to therapy" are a few examples.

Fourth Stage: Depression

Depression has just suppressed fury directed at oneself. It pertains to passive people who think they have no power to end their pain. Loss of self-worth causes depression to develop. Being in this stage is the hardest and leaves one feeling worn out and withdrawn. It is necessary to express passive rage to make it active. As a result, we can see events more objectively.

Stage Five: Acknowledgement

The stage of acceptance is not joyful. One feels emotionally depleted at this phase, as though the discomfort has passed, the fight is ended, and rest is just around the corner. Faith begins to take shape at this point, and development follows. You may start a new life.

A catastrophe may catalyze change by upending long-standing routines. Above all, you must be willing to be a healed person. You must give healing time.

Make a list of your emotional requirements and create attainable objectives for yourself. What do you want your future self to look like in a month or a year?

Conclusion

"Inner child work" is a method for locating and addressing childhood trauma. It recognizes that our childhood experiences have an impact on how we behave as adults. Reparenting ourselves is the objective of inner child therapy to satisfy our unmet needs. Self-discovery may help us better understand our routines, triggers, objectives, and requirements.

When we begin inner child healing treatment, we have access to a delicate, impressionable part of ourselves. We can be both the "grown-up" and the "kid" at the same time while yet giving steadfast support to ourselves.

You mentally and emotionally revisit that painful situation when you begin attempting to heal your inner child. You can relate to your inner child since you are an adult. Your adult self may then start to sift through the coping mechanisms your childhood self came up with to protect you from more trauma.

Your inner child may be begging you for help if you feel irritated, angry, or helpless. Realizing how your traumatic experiences impact the choices you make today might help you get out of a rut. However, it may also have a huge effect on your relationships and profession. Working on your inner child provides tremendous emotional benefits. To help people all across the globe live lives that are more passionate, clear, and meaningful, we at BetterUp work very hard. That's how kids live their lives; if not with purpose, then at least with clarity and enthusiasm.

You will always have a child's heart inside of you if it is healed. You may use these 20 proverbs to help you decide how to recover and reconnect with your inner child.

1. "Our brains gradually grow more resistant to new ideas, foolish commitments, and the surprises of the spirit" when our inner child is not nurtured and nourished

Mr. Brennan Manning

2. "I learned all I needed to know in kindergarten."

Lewis, C.S.

3. "One day, when you're old enough, you'll wish to read fairy tales once again," said Robert Fulghum.

4. A little child who is not yet much higher than they are must be as close to the grass, flowers, and butterflies as we are.

Friedrich Nietzsche

5. "Imagination is the home of our inner child, and creativity is its playground."

DeWalt, Jaeda

6. Never let your inner child go.

7. "The creative adult is the youngster who made it through."

8. "I am not my wounded inner child."

Debra Doherty

9. Accept your inner child.

Baquiran, K. A.

10. Hello, inner child; I'm the babysitter!

Pratchett, Terence

11. Remember that you periodically need to let your inner child play.
When you look after your inner child, the youngster recovers swiftly and effectively.
Andrea Beck

12. "It's important to develop your inner child. It is essential to someone's growth into a complete person.
Richardson, Cheryl.

13. "A grownup is a child in layers," someone once said.
Timber Harrelson

14. "The girl I had hidden away when I was eleven, the person I was before the world told me who to be, spoke to me for the first time that day and said, "Here I am." I'm in command now.
Craig Doyle."

15. I'm not sure whether the adult inside me is trying to educate the child within me. Instead, I think that the child is responsible for the bulk of schooling.

Lounsborough, Craig

16. "It takes courage to grow up and be who you are."

Cummings, EE

17. After some time, the middle-aged person who inhabits her head begins communicating with her spirit, the youth.

Lamott, Anne

18. "The smartest people I know are all inside like children,"

Henson, James

19. "Let's pay attention to what our inner child, who is being constrained and

imprisoned by adult society's rules, wants.
Erik Pevernagie

20. After a while the middle-aged person who lives in her head begins to talk to her soul, the kid.
Anne Lamott, Joe Jones

www.ingramcontent.com/pod-product-compliance
Lightning Source LLC
LaVergne TN
LVHW050336160826
845677LV00014B/3645

* 9 7 9 8 3 7 2 4 1 2 1 2 5 *